APPALACHIAN WOMEN

Teaching the Future

Nedra Skaggs Atwell

University Press of America,® Inc.
Lanham · Boulder · New York · Toronto · Oxford

Library of Congress Control Number: 2005929538
ISBN 978-0-7618-3300-0

Dedication

With love rooted in the past, my mother and grandmother, and hope for the future, Lauren, Lexie and Chloe....

And many thanks to all those teachers whom I have known....

Contents

Preface

Appalachian Women represents several years of reflection on the teaching and learning process. Friends and fellow educators have offered a variety of suggestions. The volume is divided into seven sections. Perhaps a brief explanation of each of these sections will assist the reader in understanding my intention.

Part One, Beginnings offers insight into my past and serves to illuminate my aesthetic development. This section is intensely personal and sets the tone for the entire work. The second part, High Expectations, discusses the value of belief in a teacher's ability to reach each student and underscores the strength found in the positive.

Teachers, the third part of the volume, considers personal qualities embodied in successful teachers. I make no apologies for believing that there are some characteristics that teachers must have innately and these cannot be taught. You cannot teach what you do not know. Language and Culture, examines the influence of developmental factors and societal bounds on the educational process.

The fifth section, Technology, is a touchstone to race to include and expand possibilities through the use of instructional technologies. Often the possibilities expand our ability to imagine. Time, Style and Assessment list many of the methods that have been proven to increase student achievement and yet are often overlooked by practitioners.

Reflections, includes the passing of the torch from one generation of teachers to those of the future. I acknowledge the contribution of my first teachers, my mother and grandmother and express my hope for the future, my granddaughters, Lauren, Lexie and Chloe.

Chapter 1: Beginnings

> **Is there ever any particular spot where one can put one's finger and say, "It all began that day"?**
>
> *~Agatha Christie*

OVER fifty years ago, in a rural remote section of Kentucky, I made my first trip to school where I learned a reverence for education and knowledge. I had teachers who taught me that knowledge was the greatest thing I could possess, that education would expand my heart, mind, and soul. When I remember those days, I am grateful for the strength and example provided by my teacher. She was the first of many special teachers I would come to know. To be a child's special teacher you must be the right kind of person, you cannot give what you do not have. We teach the fiber of our souls. We teach what we are in addition to what we know.

As I have taught and worked in public schools across Kentucky, Tennessee, and Virginia since the early 1970s, I have observed several elements that are contextually common in all of their classrooms. Without exception, these special teachers incorporate the following elements into their instructional practice: maintain high expectations for success; utilize effective praise; incorporate technology; provide direct instruction combined with challenging activities; teach metacognitive strategies; recognize and accommodate learning styles; promote self assessment and self monitoring; celebrate diversity; value and nurture parental involvement; and, protect and optimize instructional time.

Children born into a literate world where important others value reading and writing often find learning to read and write in school a relatively easy process. For many of those we teach, this is not necessarily the case. For them this process requires more attention, effort, and time. From the beginning, they find themselves challenged to learn a code and live by a set of rules they did not know even existed. Teachers help them break the code and learn the rules by reinventing their classrooms into structures that nurture and increase student achievement by incorporating the above listed elements.

According to the U. S. Department of Education, only 20% of the teachers in public schools feel comfortable (NCES 2000) with students and teaching. This is a tragedy, but can be remedied by providing them opportunities to gain a working knowledge.

Nationally, regionally, and in Kentucky, Tennessee and Virginia where I have lived, there is a critical shortage of teachers. The states report a chronic shortage of over 27,000 fully certified teachers, along with an annual demand for approximately 28,000 new teachers (NCES 2000). In greatest demand are teachers of specific learning disabilities, emotional disorders, and mental retardation (42%, 17%, and 17%, respectively, of all additional teachers needed). When considered in geographic terms, the need is greatest in rural and inner city areas (NCES 2000). The demand for teachers increases yearly, and is expected to increase at a faster rate than that of other occupations through at least the year 2009.

According to the 20th Annual Report to Congress on the Implementation of the Individuals with Disabilities Act (IDEA) (U.S. Department of Education 1998), the need for teachers has been exacerbated more by the decrease in the number of graduates in teacher education programs than by the increase in the number of students served.

Between 1987–88 and 1996–96, the numbers of general education and special education students expanded at comparable rates. However, the shortage of special education teachers during that period increased by 31%, in comparison to an increase of 14% in general education. The consistently higher rate of teacher attrition from special education intensifies this discrepancy.

The small, rural school districts characteristic of Appalachia report difficulties in attracting teachers. These districts have more than their proportionate share of these personnel needs. It is not uncommon for positions to be either unfilled or filled by personnel who were not fully certified.

The geography, culture, and economic environment of Appalachia are typical of the conditions that create difficulties for preparing, recruiting, and retraining teachers. Although teacher attrition is not necessarily greater for rural than urban schools, it is higher in schools with high percentages of poor students, and in schools where teacher pay and the resources available to teachers are low. The size of the school districts in the region varies greatly. Of these school districts, 90% have a student population under 5,000. Ninety-five percent are characterized as rural areas or small towns; only five percent are characterized as large towns or mid-size cities. Average teacher pay in the region is below the average for the rest of the state. Student eligibility for free lunch is also high in these school districts, ranging from 55% to 94%. Most of counties in the region are listed as poverty areas. Many teachers are first-generation college graduates.

The school systems in the region are usually able to hire teachers with an emergency license; however, these teachers must take courses to obtain permanent licenses. Teachers who are teaching with an emergency license, as well as teachers who wish to obtain additional endorsements, are faced with the challenge of finding a program that is affordable and convenient. The region's geography is very rural, making travel to universities difficult. Prospective teachers' professional goals may also be constrained by the need to continue to work while going to school. When I think of all of the problems faced today, I often wonder what Miss Willie would do.

Janice Holt Giles's character, Miss Willie is a favorite of mine. Miss Willie epitomizes a reflective practitioner. Her character models a mixture of passion for learning, knowledge of instructional practice, and commitment to student achievement. In many ways, Sharyn McCrumb's, Nora Bonesteel is an Appalachian sister. Nora shares the same passion for the people she loves and commitment to the things she knows; "the sight" enriches her character. Teaching requires a unique combination of the skills of both of these fictional characters.

One of the joys of my life has been my involvement with schools, teachers, parents and students across the Appalachian region. In the next several pages, please come with me as I share some of the wonders I have seen and experienced. The stories that follow are theirs. Come and share their courage and success. . . .

Chapter 2: High Expectations

> **First teach a person to develop to the point of his limitations and then–pfft!–break the limitation.**
>
> *~Viola Spolin*

TEACHER expectations effect teacher behavior, which in turn influences student achievement. Rosenthal and Jacobsen (1968) suggested that teacher expectations act as self-fulfilling prophecies because student achievement mirrors these expectations. Smiles, eye contact, opportunity to learn new more difficult material, wait time, length and number of teacher pupil interactions and feedback are tangible ways a teacher conveys the expectations she has for her students. Low expectations have been identified as one obstacle to learning (Schunk 1996).

Many teachers rise above their experiences and personal prejudices and enter an instructional relationship with the belief that all can learn and that they have the confidence and ability to teach the students they have been given. They refuse to compromise academic standards or base expectations on factors related to student performance. These teachers envision success and work to make their dreams come true.

For several years, I had the opportunity to work with schools in Eastern Kentucky as they labored to implement educational reform. At a certain point in strategic planning or working with teachers on curriculum reform, someone in the room would become discouraged and begin to complain and whine. Negative attitude is the most contagious thing on earth. If left unchecked, all it takes in any group to dampen the whole process is one or two of these toxic personalities. Schools and districts that were successful had several people that when this toxicity began would share the following personal narrative. I heard the following story with slight variations from many teachers and school administrators in Kentucky, Tennessee and Virginia.

One of the women would begin to speak in quiet tones, "Let me tell you about me. When I was a child, I loved going to school. School was the bright spot in my life. Books opened the world for me. I read about large cities with multi-story buildings that had elevators; foreign countries with different people, cultures and animals came alive; indeed the world became a wonderful place full of opportunity. I lived the lives of the characters in the books and dreamed of my future."

Then, something happened in the mines; there was a strike, illness, accident or death. The situation varied with each individual but things changed drastically at home and the always scarce resources became almost non-existent. Their role in the family increased and after a time their schoolwork began to suffer.

Invariably, their interest in school began to fade and other opportunities of the moment became brighter. For these women, the patterns followed by their mothers began to take hold. Why not leave school and marry the young man courting them? He had money, wanted to take care of them and it would be one less mouth to feed at home. They all talked of beginning to make the decision to drop out of school early or graduate and then immediately get married. Dreams of going to college or becoming a teacher were as foreign as the strange cultures and characters in the books they so enjoyed as children.

At this point, a tear would appear in the corner of their eye and their voice got softer almost reverential. Miss Sally, the name would change with each story told of these special teachers, had taken them aside and said, "Don't you do this to yourself. There is nothing wrong with what you want only the time you want it. You need to learn to be you before you become someone's wife or mother. You have the potential to do so much more. I will help you find a way to go to college. I will help and encourage you while you are in school. Do not settle for what is the path of least resistance now; you will have regrets for the rest of your life." Others within the room would begin to nod in agreement, and the tone had changed. What had seemed impossible the moment before became what would be done.

Everyone in a very personal way understood the research about high expectations. For many, the reason they became a teacher was to make a difference in the life of another. One of the greatest gifts we can give our students is an excitement and zest for learning. We need to be excited about their achievement and help provide both context and value to their accomplishments. Statements must be genuine. Students know the difference. We all need to feel valued, appreciated, and recognized.

Chapter 3: Teachers

> We do things to learn something we can
> define, and we wind up knowing things we
> never imagined even asking about.
> ~*Maxine Singer*

WHAT are the qualities of a good teacher? First, they must know their subject. That sounds simplistic and obvious but it is not always the case. This makes teaching inseparable from learning. Every good teacher will learn more about his subject every year. Teachers continue to learn so that they expand both their world and the students. The human mind is infinitely capacious. No one can begin to guess how much knowledge a student will want. A limited field of material stirs few imaginations. A subject that carries the mind out on limitless journeys, make students eager to press on.

The second quality is that a teacher must like to learn. Students dislike the insincere. A teacher who dislikes the subject or is indifferent to it runs the risk of becoming a hypocrite. However, if you do enjoy the subject, it will be exciting even when you are tired. This teacher will delight students when rested and are never at a loss for illustrations or topics for discussion. When you make a mistake, as all teachers do, admit the error and go on. You will find that you have not sacrificed the respect of your students; you will have gained it. Students do not demand omniscience. They know it is unattainable. They do demand sincerity and honesty.

The third quality of good teaching is to like students. If you do not like boys and girls, or young men and young women, give up teaching. Life is too short to be spent doing something that you do not like.

Teachers like the young because they are young. They have no faults except the ones they are asking you to eradicate. Get to know them. Know their names and faces. One of the curses of getting older is that I have begun to do this badly. If you wish to influence your students, you must get to know them as individuals but you will learn through experience that many share similar problems and learn in similar ways.

A good teacher builds bridges between the classroom and the real world. Watch teachers enjoying themselves and you will see them grow decades younger. Within each of us, lie hidden many memories, some of childhood, some of today, the good teacher draws vitality and variety from their younger memories; to know what it is to be young again without ceasing to be an adult.

The teacher will remember not only what interests her as an adult but also what used to interest her as a child. If she uses this knowledge to enrich the discussion, then the student benefits from the full life experience.

One of the most important qualities of a good teacher is humor. Obviously, it keeps students alive and attentive. The wise teacher knows that fifty-five minutes of work and five minutes of laughter are worth twice as much as sixty minutes of work. I think that one of the greatest mistakes many elementary schools are making today is the trend to cancel recess. Children need the chance to laugh, run, and play.

A teacher must have a good memory. A display of creative memory helps students in one of the most difficult jobs. Facts and bits of information learned must be connected to acquire life and grow. One way to do this is for the teacher to demonstrate how apparently remote data are linked and that sometimes happens when you least expect it.

A teacher must have perseverance. I once had a teacher tell me that I would have survived "the flood". I considered it a compliment. Think about the task of both the teacher and the student; learning takes concentration and effort.

Concentration must be learnt. It should not be thought of as nothing but an exercise of will. Concentration is an intellectual process. It is a choice. We all make choices throughout life and that which we select to concentrate upon determines the quality of our lives.

Memory and perseverance are two of the qualities that make a good teacher; another is kindness. It is very difficult to teach anything of lasting worth without kindness. Learning anything worthwhile is difficult. Some find it painful; others find it tiring.

Kindness must be genuine. Students of all ages easily and quickly detect the teacher who dislikes them. A teacher who is really interested in making a subject correctly known and understood does not expect all students to master the content on the first attempt but will help the slow and correct the confused can be considered kind. Remember, we all teach and learn all our lives.

Whatever you are teaching; make it clear. Make it as firm as rock and bright as the sun. Make it clear to those you are teaching. You must think, not what you know, but what the student does not know; not what you find hard, but what the student will find difficult. Give pictures and examples. Whenever possible, talk over with your students what you are trying to teach. A good student is seldom silent.

Anything worth learning takes time to learn and time to teach. Real teaching is not just handing out packages of information. It culminates in an actual change in the student's mind.

A teacher bears great responsibility. It is a serious thing to interfere with another's life. It can be difficult enough to guide your own. Students are influenced for good or ill when the teacher speaks with authority. The effects of bad teaching are incalculable. The rewards of good teaching are immeasurable.

Chapter 4: Language and Culture

"Don't you know cows can't fly?"
~Miss Rosemary to Gertrude

SCHOLARS have begun to look into the question of how thinking processes and cultural experiences interact in school and instructional situations. The extent of the match between home and school cultures provides a dynamic understanding of many of the variables that affect student learning and intelligence. By bringing together the works of L. S. Vygotsky, Howard Gardner, John Dewey, and Reuven Feuerstein, we can begin to develop a contextual framework for understanding language, cognition, culture, human development, intelligence, teaching and learning.

Learning can best be described as an activity requiring the construction of knowledge. Our social lives are major products of culture and the building blocks of cognition. Social experience is inseparable from thought. Moment by moment we construct our reality. This process of construction, and the understanding it provides, depends upon our previous understanding and social experiences, our culture. There is a distinct relationship between the learner and the embedded context. These contexts interweave, and by following the connections, we begin to understand the relationships among culture, language and cognition.

Sternberg (1998) proposes three intelligences in human cognition: (1) Analytical intelligence is the ability to analyze and evaluate ideas, solve problems and make decisions; (2) Creative intelligence involves going beyond what is given to generate novel and interesting ideas; and (3) Practical intelligence is the ability that individuals use to find the best fit between themselves and the demands of the environment.

The three intelligences comprise what Sternberg calls Successful Intelligence: "the integrated set of abilities needed to attain success in life, however an individual defines it, within his or her sociocultural context." The reader finds all three in *The Cow Who Wouldn't Come Down* by Paul Brett Johnson in both Miss Rosemary and Gertrude, the cow.

Sternberg argues not only that intelligence is a developing and context dependent notion, but also that traditional measures of intelligence such as IQ tests capture only a part of what it means to be intelligent, which he defines as the ability to adapt flexibly and effectively to the environment. More than mere analytical ability, humans need creative and practical abilities to succeed in their life pursuits.

To measure practical intelligence, Sternberg relies on a concept called tacit knowledge (Sternberg et al. 2000). As the name implies, tacit knowledge is knowledge that is hard to express in words. Sternberg posits three characteristics of tacit knowledge that are particularly applicable to Appalachian culture and cognition: (1) It is procedural rather than factual, which means it is knowledge about how to do something rather than knowledge about something; (2) It is usually learned without the help of others or explicit instruction; and (3) It is knowledge about things that are personally important to the learner.

Sternberg (2000) has developed domain-specific tests of tacit knowledge that are based on situations that an individual might face in the real world. Those who answer more like experts and leaders in their fields are judged to have acquired more tacit knowledge in that domain. Sternberg has argued that tacit knowledge tests are better predictors of career success than measures of genius or at least the best secondary predictors of career success after considering genius. People who are more skilled at acquiring tacit knowledge, he asserts, do better in a variety of fields including sales, business management, academic psychology, and military leadership. Appalachian women have finely tuned cognitive abilities that require the acquisition of tacit knowledge.

If the language and culture of the home, does not match the language and culture of the school there is an immediate dissonance. As language skills develop, a child's cognitive process becomes more independent. Language development allows the children ultimately to gain control over their own cognitive processes. Educational practices that ignore or negatively regard a student's language and culture could quite possibly have an adverse affect on the student's cognitive development.

Educators desire teaching that does more than impart rote knowledge and skills. Knowledge and skills are important, but real teaching involves far more, helping students understand, appreciate and grapple with important ideas while developing a depth of understanding concerning a wide range of issues. In classrooms, daily teaching events are structured around teacher-student dialogues.

Typically, the teacher asks a question or requests a student response. The student then replies. Finally, the teacher evaluates the student's response and may request further elaboration. In Johnson's book, Miss Rosalie grapples with how to control Gertrude and Gertrude seeks to exert her independence.

Effective instructional discourse and the use of instructional conversation have been demonstrated to be highly relevant to the broader linguistic, cognitive and academic development required to exhibit intelligence. For many of the students these conversations provide the context from which instruction flows. Taking advantage of natural interactions free from the didactic characteristics of formal teaching, these structured interactions are interesting and engaging. They center on an idea or concept, allow the focus to shift as the conversation evolves, but always keep the concept discernable. They allow for an active high level of participation without domination by any one individual, particularly the teacher. Students are engaged in extended interactions with the teacher and among themselves.

In instructional discourse, teachers and students are responsive to what others say so that each statement builds upon, challenges or extends a previous one. Strategically, the teacher presents provocative ideas or experiences. The teacher clarifies or instructs when necessary but does so without interfering or prohibiting the development of ideas. Teachers must learn when to prod, coax, probe or expand student input without losing momentum and interest. The teacher manages to keep everyone engaged in a substantive and extended interaction, weaving individual comments into a larger tapestry of talking, thinking and learning.

Such discourse is similar to interactions that take place between children and adults. These interactions are very important for children's learning and cognitive development. One researcher (Rogoff 1990, 157) notes that middle-class adults tailor their responses to children, "focusing their attention, and expanding and improving the children's contributions." Although not designed to teach in a formal sense, these tailored responses, Rogoff concludes, "appear to support children's advancing linguistic, thinking, and communicative skills." If we are teaching children that have not had these experiences, then teachers must provide similar experiences for them in their classrooms.

What characterizes good classroom discourse? What are its constituent elements? What must teachers know and do in order to implement these types of learning interactions with their students? Instructional discourse requires the teacher to be more of a facilitator, building upon the student's existing knowledge, guiding student learning through extended verbal interactions. Teachers encourage the development of many differing ideas based on information provided by students. Students develop a depth of thinking and give fewer single right answer responses. Increased student involvement and guided understanding establish a common foundation for cognition and language development.

Children will use language in ways that reflect their cultural and social environments. A comprehensive understanding of instructional interaction must take into consideration the cognitive and linguistic attributes of that interaction. Social context will determine the specific linguistic and metalinguistic information important for the development of language, the specific rules for social use of language, and the role assigned to language.

The elements of instructional discourse include thematic focus, activation and use of schemata, direct teaching, complex language and expression, probes for positions, fewer single right answer questions, responsivity to students, challenging but nonthreatening environment, and increased participation and motivation. The teacher selects a theme or idea to serve as a starting point for focusing discourse and has a general plan for how the content will unfold. The discourse is characterized by multiple, interactive, connected turns; succeeding conversations building upon previous ones. Background knowledge and schema provide hooks for understanding the content and expanding the cognitive process. Teachers promote cognitive expansion through the use of pictures, visualizations, and any material that supports the student's assertion. Without overwhelming the student, the teacher probes by asking, "How do you know?" "What makes you think that?" "Show us where it says that."

Much of the discourse centers around questions and answers for which there might be more than one correct answer. While having a plan and maintaining coherence of the discourse, the teacher is also responsive to the student's statements and alert to any opportunity they may provide to expand thinking and language development. Using a zone of proximal development, a challenging environment is balanced by a positive affective climate. The teacher is more a collaborator than an evaluator and creates an atmosphere that allows students to negotiate and construct the meaning of the content in a challenging and living classroom.

The curious world and the students themselves should be the center of the curriculum. Teachers must make connections between the liveliness of their student's cultural heritage and the formal language of the classroom. Children's interweaving of language, culture and cognition does pose developmental challenges, since eventually, children must differentiate and gain control over the unique interactive powers of their domains. Discourse is important to help students reflect upon their own metacognitive development. One can nurture this process; it cannot be forced. This developmental process occurs gradually and in its own time.

The complexity of development is linked to the whole of children's symbolic repertoire. Written language, unlike oral language, involves the use of a deliberately controlled system of symbols. Linguistic, cognitive and cultural characteristics of the child develop simultaneously and are interrelated. Cognitive factors may act to influence linguistic and social development. Linguistic development may in turn act to influence social and potential cognitive functioning. The development of social and cultural competence directly influences the acquisition of linguistic and cognitive repertoires. Changes in any of these domains may be attributed to changes in the other domains, and in turn may further alter the character of the individual child. This and other similar conceptualizations of integrated development should guide our instructional efforts for children, but they are particularly important as a foundation for enhancing the cognitive development of our Appalachian student population.

The human mind is a library of symbols shaped by inherited mental structures and by representations of the world that come from our own individual experiences. The cognitive processes by which we acquire knowledge develop in conjunction with cultural background and sociocultural influences. To be effective, teaching and learning practices must consider the interactions of language, culture and cognition.

Knowledge is constructed in a social or cultural context. Learning occurs in an interaction between individuals and an embedded context. Because children use language in a sociocultural context to construct meaning, language and culture function as significant tools for cognitive development. Children whose language and culture do not match those of the schools are forced to adjust their schema or to construct new schema. Such negation of a child's culture also negates the child's cognitive tools and can seriously hinder cognitive development.

Instructional discourse is a teaching strategy that is structured to take advantage of natural and spontaneous interactions between the teacher and the students and among students. The teacher transmits knowledge by modeling, acts as a facilitator and builds on prior cultural knowledge and schema to guide cognitive development and learning.

Just as Miss Rosemary and Gertrude would not give up, Appalachian women will not give up in their struggle to make their world a better and brighter place for the future. Daily they strengthen their tacit intelligence and use what is at hand to shape the environment in which they live and raise their families. The strength, courage and intelligence of these women are an example to us all.

Chapter 5: Technology

FOUR different types of technology usage have emerged based on my observations of others and my own teaching. Technology usage can serve as a knowledge source, data organizer, information presenter or facilitator.

Many lessons reflect the use of the World Wide Web (WWW). This was characterized by the identification and use of pre-determined websites. Students were instructed to access the necessary information, and guided by activity sheets, documented responses to the questions provided.

The Internet was not the only technology employed in providing content knowledge during microteaching activities. Some teachers include audiotapes in their teaching activities; others used videotapes. Teachers report feelings of freedom, since they no longer have to be the sole source of information. Students can engage with technology and be very active participants in their own learning process.

There was a heavy reliance on the technology to provide the content knowledge for the lessons. The teachers primarily used technology to reinforce or deliver traditional modes of instruction in a more efficient manner. Thus, the learner involvement became one of reading and writing the information that was then used in group question and answer sessions. Teachers are comfortable with this aspect of technology; often, stating it allows them to provide accurate information to their students while being physically engaged in other aspects of the lesson such as management.

Many lessons involved collection of numerical data. Some teachers used technology in the form of spreadsheets or databases to organize data, but showed weaknesses in their ability to integrate the development of graphic skills and authentic mathematics-related content into their lessons. These lessons typically involved small groups collecting and inputting numerical data, which then was compiled into a whole class document. If teachers are not careful, students can become passive observers while the teacher manipulated the program and constructed bar graphs from the data.

Many teachers noted that using technology to compile and project the whole group data was a worthwhile addition to the lessons' development. With elementary children, teachers noted that students needed more guidance.

While collecting and inputting facilitated observation of whole class data, teachers showed weaknesses in their ability to involve the class in data analyses and in the use of other skill such as extrapolating and making predictions from trends and or patterns indicated. In some situations, teachers struggled with translating the data from the tabulated information to the appropriate graphs, and showed weaknesses in their graphing skills and their abilities to manipulate various programs in graph construction. Often their students would step forward to help demonstrate that there were many levels of technology skill in any given situation. When actually teaching the lessons, sometimes the teachers were confused by data analysis and graphing of continuous versus discrete data.

Information presentation is the most common use of technology among the teachers during their microteaching activities. Many of them use the computer as a glorified overhead projector; paying special attention to fonts, colors and transitions. While presentation software lends itself to nonlinear forms of communication, many teachers utilized it in a linear lecture-based fashion. Students learned how to develop PowerPoint presentations and were able to vary sound and colors and to import images. In most cases, hands-on activities incorporated into the lesson and attempts were made to develop skills. However, the technology was used for information presentation and subsequent fact recall. If teachers were not careful, preoccupation with the technology can overtake the content of the presentation.

PowerPoint and Inspiration are two programs that show promise in use with students struggling with reading and writing. Both programs allow students with minimal written skills to present information in a polished format. Students having trouble with sequencing find this very useful. Teachers need to be given multiple opportunities to use both software programs.

Active involvement in learning is a hallmark of successful teaching. Many advocate that learning as inquiry can/should be a central goal for students and this will not happen if students memorize facts in isolation. It can be met only when teachers and students frequently engage in active inquiries that allow them to raise questions, define issues, collect data, analyze and draw conclusions based on evidence. In some lessons, teachers used technology to facilitate the inclusion of a number in these skills. After multiple chances to incorporate these skills, most of the students achieved this level of technology use.

Teachers recognize and use technology as an integral component in facilitating inquiry. For example, they would include digital images of what they were studying. These images would be projected via presentation software and form the basis of the following discussions. Students would then be instructed to observe, talk among themselves about their observations and to recognize and construct explanations. Their responses were solicited in a whole group discussion and the teachers facilitated higher order thinking skills as they interacted with their students. At the end of the lesson, the image is used again and students are required to write their own explanation of the occurrence.

Teachers are infusing technology into their classroom practice and these teachers are reporting that they have seen the value of technology in their own learning and are generalizing the practice to their students. Fostering the development of technology savvy teachers is possible. The experiences these teachers are having, serve to encourage technology integration within the context of their content lessons. While weaknesses are evident, reasonable progress is being made and they are overcoming their anxiety as observed beginners. Teachers engaged in the use of technology, as a teaching tool, develop new perspectives on the instructional uses of technology. These teachers are comfortable and knowledgeable in their use of technology as a tool to facilitate student learning. Integrating technology into their instructional practice gives teachers the opportunity to work through experiences and gain familiarity with the process. Miss Willie and Nora Bonesteel would be pleased.

Chapter 6: Time, Style and Assessment

To know one's self is wisdom.
~Minna Antrim

TEACHER-controlled content steps, extensive student practice, frequent feedback, rapid pacing and whole group settings characterize direct instructional approaches. Although there is evidence that direct instruction enhances the acquisition of some skills, critics argue that it can limit higher-order thinking and denies access to some students.

In classrooms, direct instruction often manifests itself as teacher-directed drill on phonics, vocabulary, spelling and basic computational mathematics. Direct instruction is a part of a larger repertoire of strategies; it is only one tool, not the whole tool kit. Successful teachers combine pedagogical approaches to increase student achievement. Projects, student-centered approaches, problem-based simulations and experiential learning are balanced and integrated into a set of challenging activities and assignments. These teachers are not obsessed with one single model or mastery of discrete skills without any applicable context. Skills are mastered in the context of their application. Opportunities are provided for higher-order thinking to strengthen transference.

Teachers provide concrete experiences to facilitate and enhance skill concept and acquisition. Field trips, demonstrations, guests and multimedia technologies augment student experiences. Learning is enhanced when it is personal and has relevance and meaning. School instruction is most effective when it builds on what students have learned outside of school and makes connections to real-life situations.

Cooperative learning methods share the idea that students work together and are responsible for one another's learning as well as their own (Slavin 1991; Johnson & Johnson 1987). Group rewards, individual accountability, and equal opportunity for success are essential. Student roles require clarification; the sequence of activity must be clear; and interactions must be monitored and evaluated.

Metacognition is taught. Students are guided to think about thinking and to share their thoughts with peers. How did you know that answer? What do I need to help me learn? Where do I go to get the resources that I need? The nature of questions asked by the teacher determines to some extent thinking and learning in classrooms. An important element of a student's experiential base is understanding and communicating in a way that structures comprehension. Semantic maps, word webs, and clustering vocabulary help students attend to levels of meaning. Graphic displays provide an organizational schema for information and vocabulary (Caine & Caine 1991).

Metacognitive strategies are techniques, principles, and rules that facilitate the acquisition, manipulation, integration, storage, and retrieval of information (Idol & Jones 1991). A wide range of thinking, learning and study strategies exist. Mnemonics, note-taking, self-questioning, positive self-talk, advance organizers, chunking, SQ4R (survey, question, read, reflect, recite, review) and DISSECT (discover the context; isolate the prefix; separate the suffix; say the stem; check with someone; try the dictionary) are just a few that are used to facilitate student mastery of curriculum.

Research widely documents individual differences. Teachers need to accommodate a wide range of environmental, physical, emotional, social and psychological conditions. In the context of instructing students, learning styles refers to the set of instructional conditions that facilitate a specific student's academic progress. Group size (one-on-one with teacher; one-on one with peer; small group; whole group), distraction management (headset, seating carrel), lighting, and room temperature can affect student performance. Learning schedules including time of day (morning, noon, afternoon, evening, night, late night) and length of lesson (10 minutes, 30 minutes, 1 hour) must be considered.

Necessary adjustment of materials (highlighting essential content, varying sequence) and aids (organizers, checklists, peer tutors) are easily implemented in classrooms. Students who are actively engaged in lessons learn more and master content more quickly. Some students learn skills and develop concepts by doing rather than merely watching or listening. Hands-on interactive approaches heighten the senses and provide a reason and desire to learn. Active learning promotes attention and increases on-task behavior.

Many of these teachers involve students in planning and evaluating learning experiences. Students develop a sense of ownership, a pride in their contribution, and personal empowerment. For many students, this leads to a holistic, integrated approach. Speaking, reading, writing, and listening are common to all academic skill acquisition and demonstration. A more integrated approach offers opportunities for review, repetition, application, and generalization of content.

One of the ultimate goals of teachers is to develop independent learners. Teachers want students to monitor and manage their behavior, to comprehend concepts and master concepts and skills empowering them to control themselves now and in the future. To help students acquire these skills, teachers encourage their students to verify the meaning of what is heard, said, read, or written. Do I need to reread? Is that sensible?

Graphic organizers assist students in monitoring school activities. Checklists assist in determining the need to reread, edit assignments, conduct experiments, and follow classroom rules. Teachers guide their students to manage attention, on-task behavior, peer and teacher interactions, and academic goals. Ask students to step back from the situation, assess the event, reflect on the feelings and interactions, and keep records. Give students the opportunity to practice and monitor behavior and learning.

Teacher interest and enthusiasm are essential to the development of student motivation to learn. Teacher enthusiasm is contagious. By efficiently managing the instructional process, teachers model self-management and self-assessment. Structuring a positive classroom environment increases teacher enjoyment and the possibility that the student will enjoy learning. Teaching and learning can and should be fun!

Effective instructional management includes planning, ordering a positive learning environment, efficient time management and scheduling, appropriate instructional groupings, use and design of materials, skill with technologies, and democratic procedures. Accentuate the positive; establish routines, and alternate activities requiring movement with quiet times.

Cultural differences can place students at risk. Language and experiential differences often divide students. Teachers can emphasize the rights of all students and teach respect for diversity. Teachers provide opportunities to experience a variety of cultures and to grow as human beings. Experiencing the music, art, literature, traditions, and food of different cultures enrich our lives. We must teach students to value their cultural roots and provide the foundation for their identity. All students must have full and equal opportunities to learn and be respected.

Appalachian teachers have a wealth of cultural material to use. School experiences must be congruent with home and community. Focus on the positive features of a culture and take every opportunity to celebrate and value our differences.

Research has consistently indicated that parent and family involvement is critical to the academic success of many students. Parents can and often want to be a teacher's greatest ally. They can and will work with teachers to enhance their child's personal, social, and academic well-being.

Parental involvement includes both home-based and school-based activities. Home-based activities involve school related tasks that are conducted at home by parents, such as reading to their child, and must be designed to be meaningful and accomplishable. School-based activities require the parent to enter the school or classroom to assist with program delivery.

Teachers must be skillful in increasing both informal and formal communicating with parents. Communication must be two-way and requires openness and parity. Casual chats, personal notes, parent-teacher conferences, newsletters, and report cards have direct cognitive and behavioral benefits.

Chapter 7: Reflections

There is no end to what you can accomplish if
you don't care who gets the credit.
Florence Luscomb

MOST teachers will recognize that many of these elements are present in their daily classroom practices. The observations I have shared are a partial summary of sound pedagogy in our complex contemporary society. Names have been changed to protect confidentiality for students and identities of teachers.

For many students, learning is so natural that mastery of curriculum, with a moderate amount of teaching is virtually guaranteed. For other students, school learning does not always appear to be natural or spontaneous. For these students, concise pedagogy is critical. Teachers cannot make assumptions. Teachers enter the instructional relationship well prepared and eager to apply the best pedagogy and processes. These teachers have an insiders understanding of their culture and communities; and they are armed with knowledge of cognitive development and posses the emotional strength to facilitate their students' progress toward educational achievement. Indeed, I can imagine these teachers linked to the past and bridging the future, a long line of strong, courageous, knowledgeable and committed women.

References

American Council of Education. 1999. *To touch the future: Transforming the way teachers are taught: An action agenda for college and university presidents.* Washington, D. C: American Council of Education.

Bloom, B. 1976. *Human characteristics and school learning.* New York: McGraw-Hill.

Caine, R. N., and G. Caine. 1991. *Making connections: Teaching and the human brain.* Alexandria, VA: Association of Supervision and Curriculum Development.

Churma, M. 1999. *A guide to integrating technology standards into the curriculum.* Upper Saddle River, NJ: Merrill.

Clark, C. S. 1995. Parents and schools. *CQ Researcher* 5: 40–69.

Dewey, J. 1916. *Democracy and education: An introduction to the philosophy of education.* New York: Macmillan.

_____. 1921. *Reconstruction and philosophy.* London: University of London Press.

Feuerstein, R. 1980. *Instrumental enrichment: An intervention program for cognitive modifiability.* Glenview, IL: Scott, Foresman & Company.

Fried, R. 1995. *The passionate teacher: A practical guide.* Boston: Beacon Press.

Garcia, E., and B. McLaughlin. 1995. *Meeting the challenges of linguistic and cultural diversity in early childhood.* New York: Teachers College Press.

Gardner, H. 1983. *Frames of mind: The theory of multiple intelligences.* New York: Basic Books.

Goleman, D. 1995. *Emotional intelligence.* New York: Bantam Books.

Henson, K.T. 1995. *Curriculum development for educational reform.* New York: Harper Collins.

Idol, L., and B. F. Jones, eds. 1991. *Educational values and cognitive instruction: Implication for reform.* Hillsdale, NJ: Lawrence Erlbaum Associates.

Johnson, D. W., and R. T. Johnson. 1987. *Learning together and alone.* Englewood Cliffs, NJ: Prentice Hall.

Johnson, P. B. 1993. *The Cow Who Wouldn't Come Down.* New York: Orchard Books.

Kentucky Department of Education. 2001. *Comprehensive System of Personnel Development* (CSPD). Retrieved from http://kydoe.ed.gov/htm.

National Council for Accreditation of Teacher Education (NCATE). 1997. *Technology and the new professional teacher: Preparing for the 21st century classroom.* Washington, D.C.: National Council for Accreditation of Teacher Education.

National Center for Educational Statistics (NCES). 2000. *Teacher education: A report on the preparation and qualification of public school teachers.* Retrieved September 2003 from http://nces.ed.gov/pubs2000/2000080.htm.

Rogoff, B. 1990. *Apprenticeship in thinking: Cognitive development in social context.* Oxford, UK: Oxford University Press.

Rosenthal, R. and L. Jacobson. 1968. *Pygmalion in the classroom: Teacher expectation and pupils' intellectual development.* New York: Holt, Rinehardt & Winston.

Schofield, J. W. 1995. *Computers and classroom culture.* Cambridge: Cambridge University Press.

Schunk, D. H. 1996. *Learning theories.* 2d ed. Englewood Cliffs, NJ: Prentice Hall.

Slavin, R. E. 1990. *Cooperative learning: Theory, research, and practice.* Englewood Cliffs, NJ: Prentice Hall.

Sternberg, R. J. 1998. Abilities are forms of developing expertise. *Educational Researcher* 27(3): 11–20.

Sternberg, R. J., G. B. Forsythe, J. Hedlund, J. A. Horvath, R. K. Wagner, W.M. Williams, et al. 2000. *Practical intelligence in everyday life.* Cambridge: Cambridge University Press.

Sternberg, R. J., & E. L. Grigorenko. 2000. *Teaching for successful intelligence: To increase student learning and achievement.* Arlington Heights, IL: Skylight Professional Development.

United States Department of Education. 1998. *20th Annual Report to Congress on the Implementation of the Individuals with Disabilities Act* (IDEA).

Vygotsky, L. S. 1929. The problem of the cultural development of the child. *Journal of Genetic Psychology* 36: 414–434.

_____. 1956. *The genesis of higher psychological functions.* Moscow: Academy of Pedagogical Sciences.

_____. 1981. The genesis of higher mental functions. In *The concept of activity in Soviet psychology*, edited by James V. Wersch (Armonk, NY: Plenum).

About the Author

Nedra Skaggs Atwell began her teaching career in Tennessee in 1972. She continued her studies in education at Western Kentucky University, where she was awarded a MAE in Exceptional Education, and Vanderbilt University, earning a Doctorate in Educational Leadership and School Administration.

For the past thirty-three years, Dr. Atwell has lived in Kentucky, Tennessee and Virginia. She has worked with K-12 schools, state departments of education, and served on the faculties of Virginia Intermont College, Radford University, and Western Kentucky University. She now lives in Bowling Green, Kentucky where she continues teaching and working with schools.

www.ingramcontent.com/pod-product-compliance
Lightning Source LLC
Chambersburg PA
CBHW030657270326
41929CB00007B/410